731
RIE

C. 1

Rieger, Shay

The bronze zoo

DATE			
MAY 5 1973 507			
MAY 30 1972 506			
MAR 20 1975 506			
Osborne			
Delnoce			

DRAWN

THE BRONZE ZOO

by Shay Rieger

Charles Scribner's Sons   *New York*

acknowledgments

Miss Gladys V. Thorne, Director, Minisink Town House, New York City Mission Society; Mr. Edgar Tafel, Architect; Mr. and Mrs. Joseph H. Hirshhorn, The Joseph Hirshhorn Collection; Mr. and Mrs. R. H. Shepherd, Connecticut; Mr. N. Lushington, Director, Greenwich Library, Greenwich, Connecticut.

Special thanks to Mr. and Mrs. Ted Wilentz; Mr. Abraham Glasser; and Miss Denise Hicks; to John and Robert Spring of The Modern Art Foundry; also to the Renaissance Art Foundry.

Photographs by Eeva. Courtesy of the American Museum of Natural History, the Bronx Zoo, and the Central Park Zoo.

To Holly and Adam

When you touch sculpture, it touches
you back.

—David, age 10

I think sculpture should be outdoors
in the fresh air, then we can always
say "hello"!

—Alice, age 9

introduction

The first time I saw sculpture I was seven years old. A teacher took our class to the museum. We saw beautiful Italian figures in marble. They were life-size, with every detail of their features and their clothes carved perfectly. Most of the sculptures were roped off from us while others were enclosed in dusty glass cases. The teacher kept telling us "Don't touch!" and the museum guards stood by to make sure that we didn't.

The only outdoor sculptures I saw as a child were those in the park. They were usually monumental bronze statues of some general on horseback. They looked even more immense and distant because they stood on high pedestals. For a long time sculpture seemed to me to be a thing out of reach that had nothing to do with our daily lives.

Maybe it was because of that first museum, I was particularly happy when I was asked to do bronze sculptures for a garden in Harlem—in New York City—and for a country garden in Connecticut. The site chosen for the sculpture in the city was perfect—right in front of the entrance to a community center, where hundreds of children would pass each day and be able to reach and touch the sculptures. I decided to make young animals and keep them down in size so that the youngsters could relate easily and comfortably to them.

In doing the sculptures for the country, the problem was quite different. These animals were for a private garden with lawns, trees and the sky as background. Since the sculptures would be in an open, spacious area I decided to make them life-size and larger. Here, too, they were placed so they could be reached and touched.

It took over two years to complete the Bronze Zoo.

Shay Rieger

the artist at the zoo

Before starting the sculptures I visit the zoo. I am planning to make a hippopotamus, a camel, and an elephant for the city garden in Harlem; then, whooping cranes, aardvarks, giraffes, and an ostrich and a yak for the garden in Connecticut.

the camel

I often do quick pen-and-ink sketches, using just a few lines to suggest the forms and features I want to remember later.

This camel at the Bronx Zoo poses proudly.

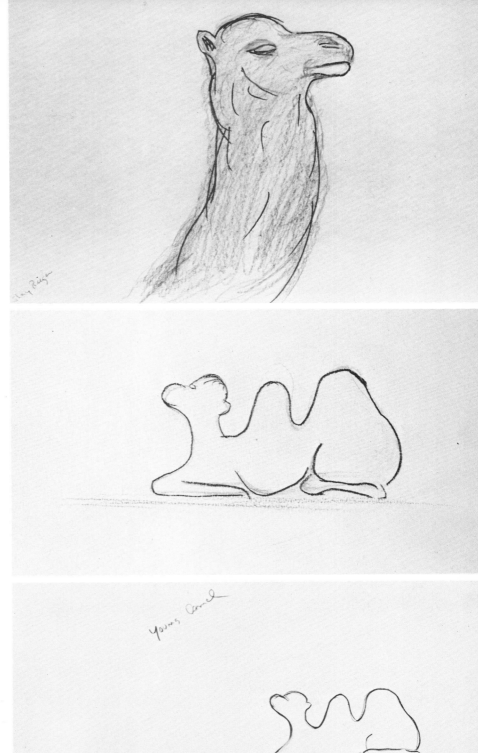

For my sculpture I will do a young camel in this resting position.

the elephant

This is an Indian elephant. His back is arched and his ears are smaller than the African elephants, which have large ears and concave backs.

Again, a few lines tell me what I want to remember about the elephant. I think of how I will express in sculptural terms the animal's huge bulk and features, his trunk and floppy ears.

I decide to make my sculpture from this sketch of a young elephant lying down.

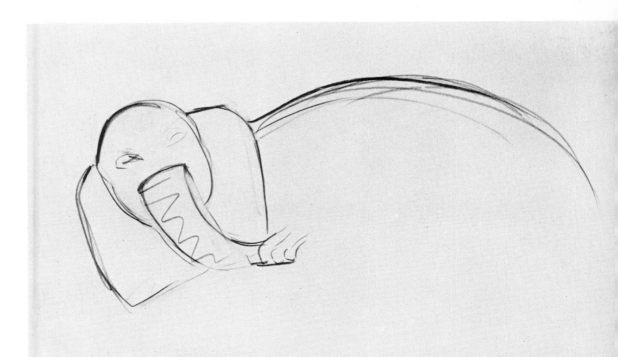

the hippopotamus

This is the beautiful young hippo I used as my model. She is two years old and weighs six hundred pounds.

...And she poses very nicely.

These are sketches of the hippo that I will take back with me to my studio.

In this one I used an ink wash to remind me of the hippo's massive shape.

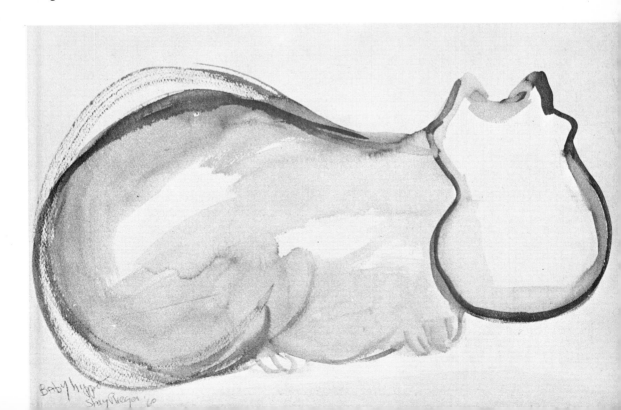

Baby hippo
Shay Vega '60

the clay hippo

Later, in the studio, I begin the sculpture. With the moist, pliable clay I mold the hippo, keeping the sketches nearby.

While I am working on the clay I keep in mind that the final form will be bronze. I want the finished bronze to express my sense of the hippo as a heavy, earth-bound creature.

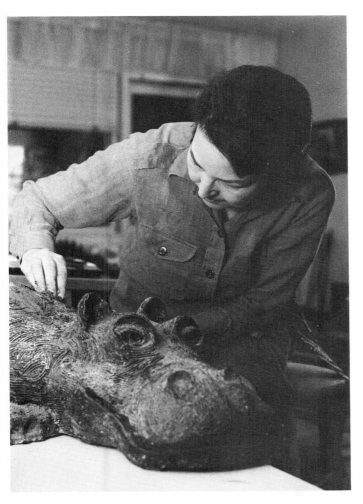

The hippo has taken shape, with its features defined.

It took four weeks to finish the clay hippo, and many more weeks to do the camel and elephant in clay.

at the foundry

This is where the clay models are cast into bronze. Since this is done by a very special technique called the *lost wax* process, most sculptors do not do this work themselves. It is done by trained workers at the foundry.

The clay sculpture of the hippo has been delivered to the foundry. Making it into bronze involves many stages. One of the most important steps is making a wax reproduction of the clay model.

the wax hippo

First, a rubber mold is made by pouring liquid rubber over the clay. When the rubber sets, it hardens into an exact impression of the clay hippo. In this picture the foundryman is finishing the rubber mold.

The next step is to pour hot, molten wax into the rubber mold.

The men pour off the excess wax, leaving a thin layer inside which will harden into the shape of the clay model.

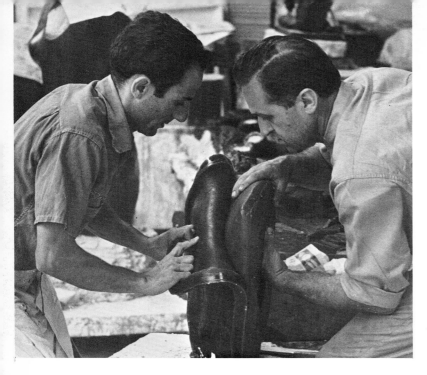

The men are pulling the rubber mold off the hardened layer of wax.

The wax is just like the clay hippo except that it is hollow inside.

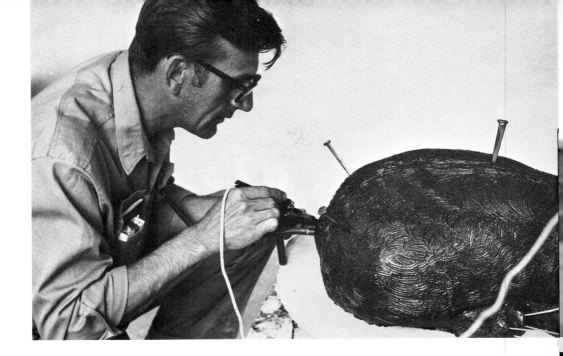

Wax tubing is set into the form to make *gates* and *air vents*. The *air vents* are for air and gases to escape when the hot molten bronze is poured. The *gates* allow the bronze to run into the mold.

The tubing in the mouth will be the opening for the pouring of the metal. The toothpicks are put in to make still more air vents, and the nails hold the mold together.

throwing the investment

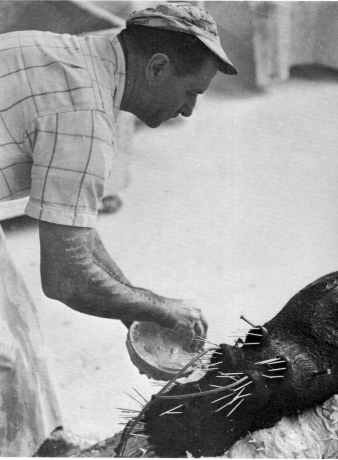

After it is sprayed with a solvent the wax hippo is ready to be given a plaster and silica covering. This mixture is called the *investment*. It can withstand heat and will not burn away. The spray helps it stick to the wax model.

A foundryman begins to throw the investment. It looks and feels like heavy cream and hardens quickly. It is also put inside the wax hippo to act as a core so that the bronze cast will be hollow.

Now nearly all covered, the wax hippo is encased in a block like a mummy except for the opening on top for pouring the bronze.

pouring the bronze

This oven is called a kiln. The wax hippo—in the plaster block, or mold—is placed inside the kiln at a 1,000-degree temperature. The heat melts away the wax, which runs out, leaving a space in the mold that is the exact shape of the hippo. It is into this space that the bronze will be poured.

Into the top opening of the mold the men are pouring the hot, molten bronze. The temperature for molten bronze is 2,000 degrees.

The metal is now a liquid, but will cool and harden in a few hours.

The foundryman breaks the mold to free the bronze inside. The plaster core will also be broken and shaken out to make the sculpture hollow.

The bronze hippo has emerged, but with some burrs and rough spots. A worker removes them with an electric file. This is called *chasing*.

Now for the final touch—a little patina (color) and a coat of wax— and the hippo is ready to be sent to the Harlem garden. Along with the hippo will go the camel and the elephant, which were also cast in bronze at the foundry.

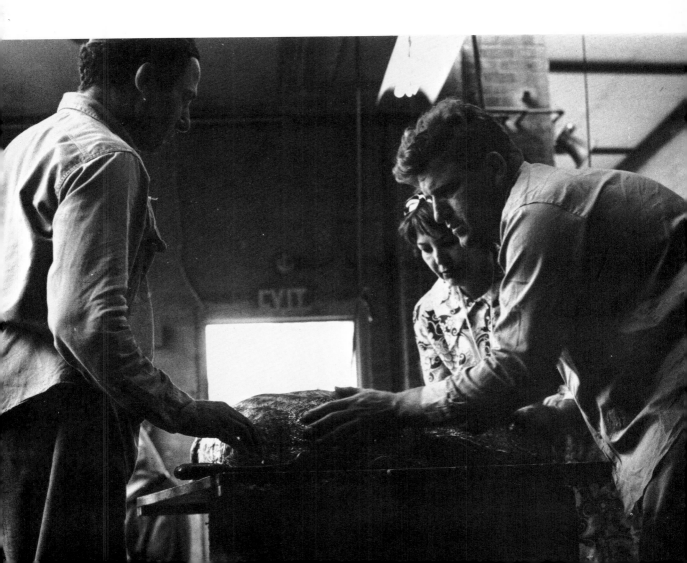

the dedication of the garden in Harlem

At a dedication ceremony the animals are welcomed to the community.
Here the camel, elephant, and hippo have been set in a cement base
and become a permanent part of the garden.

A closer look at the young hippo. . . In the final bronze it looks exactly like the clay model, down to the lines cut in the surface that give it texture and expression.

The elephant and camel against the city background. . . They have also been faithfully reproduced from the original clay.

please touch

and sit

and climb

The bronze zoo for the city garden is finished. It has been a happy experience to have the sculptures that started out from sketches at the zoo become part of the city-scape. The bronze material and natural shapes of the animals against the brick buildings complement each other. And the sculptures are now a part of the community's daily life.

the animals for the country

For the country I first plan to make the whooping cranes, then the aardvarks, giraffes, ostrich, and yak. Since there are no whooping cranes at the zoo I have to look for them at New York's Museum of Natural History.

At the museum I find these mounted specimens. It is sad to know that the graceful white crane is nearly extinct. There are only about sixty-five left in the world.

Here is a sketch of the group of cranes in the different positions I plan for the sculptures. Because of their slender necks and legs I will mold them differently from the way I did the hippo, camel, and elephant. They will have a special structure for support.

building plaster cranes

At the studio, with the sketches and my impressions of the cranes, I begin the work of sculpture. On the wall are tools I will be using.

This structure of pipes and chicken wire is called an *armature*. It is the framework, or skeleton, on which I will build the sculpture.

I am covering the *armature* with plaster.

Unlike clay, plaster hardens rather quickly and will stick to the pipes and chicken wire as I build up the form. In this picture I am putting on the plaster with my hands. When it hardens, I carve it with chisels and files.

After many months I have finished the cranes. Here, I am setting in the wooden sticks to support their delicate legs. This is necessary for shipping them to the foundry.

The cranes are made smooth with files and sandpaper.

The plaster models will be cast in the same way as the clay hippo.

When I began making the cranes I thought of them in a group for the country setting. The cranes are like a family.

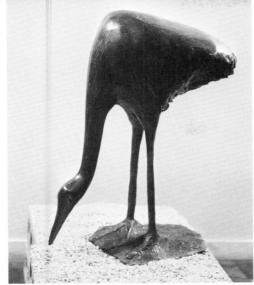

the bronze cranes

Here is the baby crane cast into bronze. He is bending over sniffing the ground, very curious about the world around him.

This one is like the mother.

This is the father crane who stretches his head high and stands alert and protective of the others.

And the other young crane. . . Before they are put in the garden I will make the other animals for the country.

the aardvarks

Aardvarks are unusual animals right down to their name. They are termite eaters from Africa. They have ears that resemble those of a donkey, and snouts like a pig's. They have long, tapering tails and strong claws for digging.

These are my sketches of a mother and baby aardvark that I made at the Museum of Natural History.

Baby Aardvark 1968

The aardvarks, too, were first made in plaster. When the bronze aardvarks are put in the country garden they look very natural there —searching for ants and termites.

the giraffes

At the Bronx Zoo this giraffe is much taller than the twelve-foot fence.

For my sculpture I am doing two giraffes, so I draw a pair of them, making one a little taller than the other. From these sketches I then build the sculptures with plaster on *armatures*—like the cranes.

In this picture they have been cast in bronze and put in the country garden. Notice how I have suggested their body pattern by chiseling chopping marks in the sculptures.

Through summer and winter these bronze giraffes overlook the landscape in Connecticut.

the ostrich

While I was at the Bronx Zoo I saw this ostrich. The ostrich is the largest of all birds. His wings are not big enough to raise his body from the ground. But he can outrun many animals, and also uses his powerful legs to defend himself by kicking.

Here I am trying to get a close look at a young ostrich.

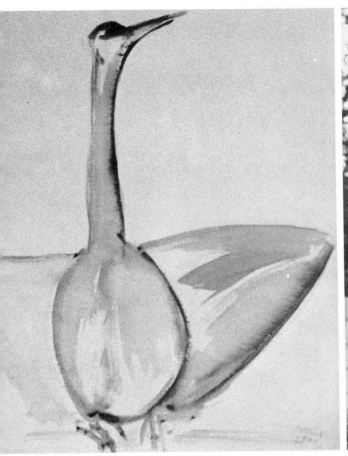 

This is my sketch of the ostrich. Again, I built the sculpture on an armature.

I did the feathers by making rough, uneven patterns of markings around the wings and body. The bronze ostrich is pictured here in the country garden—where he can spread his wings!

the yak

Although he comes from far-away Tibet, this yak looks quite comfortable in the Central Park Zoo. Yaks are a kind of ox. In Asia and Tibet they are used as field animals and beasts of burden.

This quick sketch of a young yak helped me when I began the sculpture.

Here is the bronze of the young
yak, finished and put on a base.

His horns are brightly polished
because the children touch them
so much. When bronze is polished it glitters like gold. But
when it is outdoors and un-
touched it will gradually oxidize
and turn a gray green. This gives
some sculptures added interest.

the cranes in the country garden

The bronze zoo for the country garden is finished and the animals have taken up their residence in the Connecticut countryside. There the children can look at them and touch them—against their background of trees and sky and grass.